A Garden of my Life

Cheryl Ainsworth Martin

ISBN: Softcover   978-1-5245-1134-0
        EBook   978-1-5245-1133-3

Print information available on the last page

Rev. date: 01/25/2018

To order additional copies of this book, contact:
Xlibris
1-888-795-4274
www.Xlibris.com
Orders@Xlibris.com

The Author

This Garden

This garden is divine
In this garden there's many a vine
It is the handiwork of God,
It is the creation of the Lord,

It blooms with beauty in one accord.
It's love is here for you to afford;
Meditate and focus on your duty
And relax and take in the beauty

Of every rose and every carnation
Fill up your soul with jubilation
Forget about collecting remuneration
Fill up your mind with exhilaration

Life is about making a celebration.
Let joy enter your soul,
Color the world like a rainbow,
Let peace be on your scroll,

Let its sweetness fill your soul.
Taste the pureness in each buttercup
Let the juice of each olive
Strengthen your body and soul

And increase your love and joy
Run through the labyrinth of your being
Running past the limitation of an earthly lease
Let the garden be your hiding place

Inspiration for your race.
Let the magnificence of this garden
Spread out like the creation
of the hanging gardens of heaven.

Let the daisies run along the shrubs
Forcing you to surrender to God's amazing Grace.
Let the tulips give meaning to your struggle
And brighten your perceptions of reality.

Let the marigolds crystallize in your mind
Reinventing the supernatural forces of the God-head
Let the ferns spring and rejoice in the glory
of God's presence everywhere.

Let the sunflowers grow taller than the daily puzzlements
Of your mundane life and bear existentialisms.
Let the grapes on the vine feed your hunger
Let the juices of the apple quench your thirst
and never let you weep again.

Lord . . . let me stay in this glorious garden
Let me sit and kneel at your feet
And marvel at the beauty of your creations.
Let me expunge my worries and perplexes in this divine place
and study war no more

Let the mulberry bushes cover my questions
and my longing for truth be satisfied by my faith
In you my one and only God.

Let its roses intertwine around the foundation of love
Let the dandelions smile at you fill up the area of your mind,
Reminding you that God is in charge
AND ALL IS WELL . . .

Let the aromatic perfumes of this garden sweeten your mood
Let the flowers blossom into your unique situation.
Life will always reward you for patience and penitence

The Hanging Gardens

Today I saw the palace in Hawaii.
Today the bird is a Kiskadee.
It is sitting in its nest
In the most voluptuous hanging garden
    that there ever was.

The hanging gardens are beautiful.
They are glorious and historious.
The hanging gardens are supernatural
Only God can make a garden like this.

It is completely divine.
It is sacred and harmonious.
It is perfect and delightful
It spreads around with love and glory.

It's blessing the people and hanging without.
It is a foretaste of heaven
I want to let this garden develop, guide and nurture me.

I want to be covered in its beauty
I want to become whole and part its overflow
I want desperately to hide in there
and never come out.

These feelings are bold and beautiful
I would feel secure in there
Opulence and magnificence
Will cover me up.

The fruits will produce juice . . . .
The juice will produce sweetness.
The juice will fill my stomach with nectar.
At that time my enigmas will dwindle and disappear.

Then I will lift up my eyes unto the hills,
From when cometh my help
Oh my Lord, there is beauty all around
There is love in every nook and cranny.

I don't want to leave this garden;
Let me stay there and pray.
Amen.

4

Light Up The Fire

Light up the fire in my soul.
Light up the fire to free my soul.
Set me free, to worship Thee.
Set me free to learn from Thee.

Sometimes I'm moody and unsure
I want the fire in my soul to burn brightly
I want the light in my soul to be a burning flame
Showing everyone just who I really am.

I am praying always for peace.
I am hoping always for goodness
Every day is a new beginning
Every day is a time to start over

Every day is a time to do better.
Light the fire for all to see
To see the beauty of Jesus inside of me
Light the fire of love in my heart

Then I will receive all my blessings from above.
Show me your face
Let me have your grace
Give me courage for the crises

Let the joy of the Lord be my strength.
Let sweet songs of praise emanate from within
Let holiness be my permanent activity.
Let righteousness fall from lips like a proclivity

Let there be peace on earth and let it begin with me.
Tolerance should be my pie
Cooperation should be nigh . . .
Let me draw night by faith

Knowing that God's plans for me are success
and gladness that leads all the way to glory
I want to lift up my voice and sing
Till the earth and heavens ring—

Ring with the harmony of freedom.
Let the fountain of love
Flow down like a mighty waterfall,
And fill up the panacea with excellence and quintessence.

The Safe Room

Today I was in the safe room
Armed with a dustpan and broom
Today it was time to clean the room
Today I decided was time to get out of the room.
It was time to climb out of the cave
To climb out of the mud
To go and visit the exercise club.
Today it was time to climb out of the gloom,
Before this room becomes my tomb.
To climb up to a higher plain
To climb up to a higher grain.

Happy Thanksgiving

Every day is the right day for thanksgiving.
Every day is the right time for praising
Every praise is to our God
Every word of worship is to our God.

Every breath, every gasp is to our God
Glory and honor, dominion and power is to our God
Glory belongs to God
Magnificence belongs to God.

Beauty belongs to God
Thanksgiving belongs to God.

I Trust In God

I trust in God and not another
I praise God and not another
I raise up my voice in adoration to the King of Kings
And to the Lord of Lords

Glory. . . . Praise . . . .
How excellent is thy name in all the earth.
When I praise my God, many blessings come down;
I put all my trust in God

I will lift up mine eyes unto the hills,
from whence cometh my help,
My help, cometh from the Lord,
who made heaven and earth.

Dance before the Lord
Adoration belongs to God
Exploration belongs to God
Education belongs to God

Worship belongs to God.
Glory and honor; I ain't got time to die
Because I want to dance
Let me dance before the Lord

I want to dance for freedom
I want to dance for children — all the boys
And all the girls — Hallelujah
Glory to God in the highest,

Let me lift up Holy hands and dance.
Let coals of fire bruise my lips — but let me dance
I want to dance for victory
I want to dance for liberty

And on earth there must be peace and goodwill to ;all men
Glory, honor, dominion and power to our God Almighty
Alpha and Omega — the beginning and the end
For ever and ever Amen.

Change Is For Me

Change is for me, change is for you
And change is for everyone
Change never ends
Change is for friends
Change is something that never ends.
Change is about maturing.
Change is about procuring.
Change is about alluring.
Change is good for everyone,
Even if you are only one in a million.
Change is about shedding of the old,
And growing into the new
Change is good for you;
because you can always get your due,
but don't be blue, although it is your due.

The Promenade Gardens

Today we all went to the Promenade Gardens
We walked through rows and rows of flowers,
shrubs, bushes and vines
I saw the beauty of the earth.

I saw the glory of the earth in a cascade of colors.
There were tulips and tamarinds everywhere
There were carnations and dandelions in abundance
There were sunflowers

There were marsh dowers
There were daisies running along the fences
There were tall reeds bracing against the overgrowth.
This and all the flora and fauna made up
The beautiful promenade gardens.

One Love

You're my dove
Wear your glove
It's one love
You live in a cove
You get your pinions by the drove
We can unite
We need not fight
We need not fight.
Nothing scares me
Even death doesn't scare me
God is my father
Jesus is my Savior
The Holy Spirit is my comforter
It's "One Love".

Life Is A Circle

We are in the circle of life
Trees grow, gardens grow
What goes around, comes around
Go to the top, or touch the ground
You know that's a fact
Life is like a big circle
What comes first
the chick or the egg?
Shake a leg, shake a leg
Never, ever decide to beg
What you see, is what you get
Don't ever worry or fret
You will always get — you bet.
The color of love is always the same
in the eyes of a child
Life is one big circle.

You Light Up My Life

When I see you . . . I see me
When I look into your faces
I am thankful and amazed
because of my girls and boys.
I am full of my joy when I see you
I become ecstatic and alive
I can walk up the highest mountain
I consider my life as a fountain . . . a fountain of life.
I am filled with digits
I want to go the extra mile
I want to run and smile
I want to ponder for a while . . . on life's joys.
I am overjoyed, because you are so wonderful
You truly light up my life
You are my dear and loving grandchildren.

Ms Can Can

Ms Can Can — That what I am
I can read . . . I can write . . . I can also light — up a room
I can see . . . I like to drink tea
I can walk . . . I can talk.
Oh my, the list is quite long, because I am so strong
I can change . . . I can rearrange . . . for sure I can run the range
It's a shame, but there are so many things I can do
I do get crazy . . . But I am not hazy.
I get dizzy and sometimes frizzy;
I'm always in a tizzy

The Power of Reading

Reading is for leading
Reading is for succeeding
Reading is always the best
It can help you pass your test.

Reading is good for everyone
Reading is good for the brothers
Reading is good for the sisters
Reading is also good for the mothers.

Sisters should do it
Brothers should love it
Mothers must insist that children do it
Reading, Reading, Reading is also fun.

You can do it in the sun
You need to do it because it is also fun
Reading a book increases your mind
Even if you are deaf and blind.

It can help you sow
It can help you grow
Opening a book increases your mind
It can even teach you how to be kind.

The things you can find in a book . . . If you look
It can make you cry . . . It can make you laugh
It can make you sigh and wonder
It helps one find solutions to problems.

Don't let anything get in your way
Make time for reading every day
And you will be the brightest
And the wisest you can be

I'm Queen Hadassah

I'm a queen "Queen Hadassah"
I love to eat hassar and curry with massala
I was born for greatness
Look at me; I was born for preakness.
I have rubious lips
I have a beautiful mind that clips
I am certainly a queen
You know I am not mean.
I was born to teach

You can tell it from my speech

So let me show you the way

Let me show you where to stay

Let me show you how and where to pray.

Pray for peace

Pray for violence and hate to cease

Pray for your family's love and wealth increases

Remember I love you . . . but God loves you more.

Learn From My Life

Justlookatme
Life'sbeengoodtome
Everythingfellintoplace
Justtakeacloserlookatme.

Theseedshavebeensown
Thechildrenarenowgrown
Thebeautifulbirdshaveflown
AndtheKingisstillonthethrone.

Thedoghasgottenthebone
Thepigisstillnotafalcon
Thebabyisnotananimal
Theideaoflovingisareality

Theideaofcaringisaninterestingpasstime.
Sharingshouldbeaglobalactivity
Asacivilizednationwemustlearn
Howtocareabouteachother

Wemustlookandseeourselvesineachother.
Wemustformteams.
Wemustsaveourstreams.
Wemustfindthegoodineachother.

Wecanbringoutthebestifwelookalittlelonger
Ifwelookbelowthesurface.

The Unheralded Teacher

Get it . . . You are a throw-away teacher
Don't get vexed — You are an ATR
You're in the pod of "The Absent Teacher Reserve"
You're a teacher in excess.

"What do you mean?" I asked.
You didn't pass the test
You need to go to the west
You need to read Aris.

Youmustkeepabreast
Dancetothetwist...Catchthefiots
Whyareyourunningaround?
Justbenddownandtouchtheground.

You can't speak to the Superintendent:
The Superintendent put you in the box.
He doesn't speak to people like you, just like that
You are a stealthy fox — you are in excess .

Go online . . . you look find
Don't eat and dine and don't drink your wine
Check the sex . . . Your name is Lex
Check new site — remember to step light

Check the museum of natural history
Tell them that you are free
Call the DOE . . . Call the NSE . . . Call the ISC .
Your name is Cece . . . Call clickety, clickety,
clack

Don't turn back . . . Did you get your email
Did you read your electronic scale.
You are floating from school to blinking school
— Just get a life .

No one can put you the payroll
You need special clearance.
No one will place you, without the principal 's
approval
No one will face you without a heart revival.

Put down that walking stick
You don't have the right trick
Put it down, like yesterday
Push away, and start to pray
We don't do the feeding program in here.

ABC

A — Ask
B — Believe
C — Claim
D — Don't Swear
Show that you care
Life has fun and cheer.
Come here . . . Be near
Come closer . . . Life is to enjoy
Stay with me boy

Life is a joy.
When you stand next to me
Life like love, is a many splendored thing
That lights up my world
Like stars in the night.
Enjoy . . . Just don't go ship-a-hoy
Don't worry . . . Be happy
Everything is gonna be alright.

Hang In There

Things will fall into place
Hang in there. God is here.
Faith will hold you near
Mercy and love will always you care.
Hope serves as the instrument of alignment
Justice is our consignment
Love, for the souls of the dear
You must have, you should not be scared.
Hold on my child . . . Joy comes in the morning
Don't act wild . . . Jesus is your Savior and guide
He is also your redeemer
He will always carry you through,

I Love New York

I see a huge Christmas tree
I see a world laced hope . . .
The city of possibilities
New York City, it is nice they named it twice
New York, New York.
I can see a city of possibilities
Herein lies beauty.
It's my wonderful city
Oh, this wonderful Christmas tree
Trying its best to reach humanity.
This tree is showing the message of unity
Unity is for everybody
It's good for the boys and for the girls
Unity is good for everybody
. . . even the poor and shoddy.
Unity is fleeting, Unity is sheeting
Unity is generating love for the people of the world
I love New York . . . It is the great equalizer.

RAIN

Today is a good day to welcome the rain. . . . .
Rain is for the sane.
Rain is the balm in Gilead.
Rain is a cleanser.
Rain is a strong worker.
Flowers know the value of the rain.
Rain is the essence of life.
It is what we need to stay alive.
Let it rain; let it wash away the dust; it must.

Let it fill up the streams
Let it wet on the dry lands
Let it do its divine work
Let the cycles of life never leave out its moisture and wetness.

The dew on the vegetations and the cropations of the gardens
Rejoice at the touchings of the rain
Rain is a welcome guest
Rain fills up the vats and reservoirs .

It reminds us of God's ever lasting favor in our lives ,
Rain is the solution to our own yearnings –
To be kind and gentle with nature
Today, I refuse to be up set when it rains.

I am doing a U - turn about my perceptions –
About the natural things like Rain
Rainfalls on the plants, the animals the houses,
the savannahs, the trenches and the mountains.

This divine messenger is a friend that
we all cannot live without . . .
It washes away dross, acrimony, paper, ink, sand and soil
But we can har ness it, if we try
And try we must, as we also harness our lives .

The Wonderful Fall Season

What is there? Can you see . . .
Pictures on the wall
The things in the stall
The leaves are starting to fall
— Frosty is on call.

They walk through them all at a crawl
Raise your head; stand tall
The season is fall
On God you can always call.

The birds know it all
They all kiss and they whistle
as if they were larks
They fly around the parks
So express yourself, clear the shelves
and be prepared.

Get rid of the pain
Organize, harmonize. Never
acrimonize, synchronize
Let the butterflies rise . . . way up in to the skies
Apologize seek forgiveness and
keep your eyes on the prize.

Christmas Day Is Everyday

Everyday can be Christmas day
When you see beauty all around, that is great
When you have blessings, that is great
When you experience divine order
all day long that is really great .

Christmas can be an attitude of gratitude,
for all of life's manifold benefits
Counting blessings and being distracted
by work is all about Christmas
Today, I welcome Christ in to my life
and I want to spread the joy of
Christmas all around
The past is dead and gone
The future is bright because of Christmas day
The day our Lord and Savior
was transitioned to earth

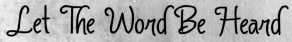

Let The Word Be Heard

Go tell it on the mountain
Over the towns and everywhere
Make the message plain
It's okay . . . we will explain.
Eat your vegetables and greens
You will not always remain a teen
Forget about your age
Use exercise too as a gauge.
Read the Word . . . I mean every page
Lift up your fellow man
Organize the wreckage
You my friend are now at that critical stage.
Everything is coming at me
Can I take it all in?
I see colors dancing around
I see words and pictures racing
to be crowned.
Lose the speed . . . Renew the creed
Simplify . . . Abilify . . . Multiply . . . Glorify

My Baby

I am very happy . . . My baby is not snappy
Look at my baby . . . She is a little lady
She is a rare gem . . . She is an awesome person
When I look at her newness . . . I see God's glory.

When I look at her smoothness
I can see the glory of God's goodness
Praise God and all the angels in heaven
Praise God for sending his only begotten son

So that my baby can enjoy everlasting life

My desire for peace is a wellspring of amazing grace
I mean it's a mighty waterfall of
God's majestic overflow
into my ordinary life
Oh, I want you to escalate with me
I want you to rise up to a higher and new standard.
Just come along with me for this copouscacious enticement.
Love calls me . . . Love beckons me . . . Love is shaking me
Love is lifting me through and through
Oh, when I think of all the possibilities of this audacious fuel.
My soul cries out - hallelujah!
Thank God for saving me
My heart resounds glory, glory
Oh, I have a story. . . Oh, what a wondrous story
I want to kick out and sail away to a new destination.
Just let me escape the limiting
Dimensions of this world of sin.
Wash out the mess, get me some rest
Let me eject all of the confusion
and turmoil that has held me down for so long
I experience it in the drudgery of this scull drudgery
Let the threshing begin
Let the straining begin
Let the scraping begin
Let the rapture begin
Take me up to a new plain
Take me up to heaven and lift me like a crane
Take me higher than a raven
I am scraven for the higher upliftment
I might be gravaliscious
I might be superstitious . . . but the bottom line remains the same
There is this bundle inside
It's eternal fire that burns within my chest
An inexhaustible combustion is going on . . . I cannot rest.
It cannot be put out
It cannot be blown out
it can't be in a pocket . . . oh no

The Love Dove

Look at me . . .
I can be whatever I want to be
Just let me be
Perhaps, I can be seen as a "Dove of Love"

I am the Love Dove.
My stuff is effervescent . . .
It is cuter than a crescent
My stuff cannot be vented

It also cannot be bent and it cannot even be sent.
My love is not for sale
It is bright and not pale
My love is a continuous tale

It is bigger than a whale.
Oh glory, what a wondrous story!
My love is an unending cory
It's filled with scory, it is celestial and it is special

It is also quintessential.
My love is more than universal
It is amazingly controversial
My love is like a tutorial

So, just jump into this sea and get soaked completely.
The sea is divinely wide and deep
It is a sea of love
Let it envelop you, you'll fit in

And you will see . . . you will not sink, but swim.
When you jump in, you will have no choice because you will change
You will see a new range
You will be soaked up in its eternal flames

These erudite flames can fan you into another world
Where there is peace and perfect love.
Those incandescent essences will run through
the voluminosity of your whole soul.

It will run through the labyrinth of your soul
like sweet medicine
It will awaken erroneous zones
where only angels can travel
peruse and dwell
Oh, just come up and take a leap of faith.
Plunge in and feel the full vigor of its vitality and clasp
Oh, just sit up
and drink from its fountain of superfluous joy
It is not a toy
This love dove is sweet.
It is better than an earthly treat.
It cannot stay in the street,
It cannot be contained in a beet
It needs to fly and flutter all around the globe
It is a mundo, it is a fundo.
It is keener than a trope
Let it hang out on a rope
It gives us all hope
It gives us all hope.
It gives us all head-of-stateness

I want this dove to alight on your minds
I want it to infuse you with its awesome powers
You can never escape its influence
I know for sure that it's electric.
It is past comprehending
It is faster than light
It is so vast, it runs past galaxies
Oh, my Lord — just ravish me with the
sweet medicines of your anointing.
Just push me out of this fixation on this mundane earth
Just propel me into that ostentatious river —
running down into my lower bowel
and regrouping the fullness of God's might.
Let me expand to the ethereal zeniths and pinnacles of might
These lessons are just super
These lessons are a cleanser
There is wealth and health in this dove of love.
It is encapsulated in its capsule
It is a rocket . . . oh yes

This love dove is a messenger.
This love dove is not a passenger
This love dove is not a messenger
This love dove is a plum line from here to eternity
It teaches you . . .
It preaches for you
It reaches up higher for you
It produces fire . . . It is a rocket....oh yes
It is not for hire . . .It's a flyer
It can dig you out of the mire
It is a carrier of untold properties and propensities
It's just this idea that we must understand
that on the underground railroad, all things a 'a possible.
I need grace
I can jump over every stumbling block when I lift up my wings
This dove can transcend cultures,
This dove can speed past time and space.
It frees you . . . It lightens you
It unleashes you . . . It liberates you

I'm fairest among those thousands of earthlings.
So many people refuse to deal with me, But truth be told,
I'm blessed I'm not stressed, I'm not oppressed,
I am confessed, I am congressed, I'm not suppressed
I'm up-fessed, I'm pressed down and running over with joy,
I'm caressed, I'm effervesced. I'm bubbling over,
I'm bolded over I'm crossing over,
I'm crossing over I'm getting it.
I'm letting it . . . I'm grazing in a new pasture,
I'm stanching in a new posture,
I'm getting closer and closer to my Lord,
I'm reconfiguring my own constellations *
I'm realigning my destiny %
I'm protruding into a new direction Just
move out and let me go through.

It is getting bigger and better,
day by day, and night by dark night.
So, I am here I may be near, I may be in the rear

I am going in the new direction of hope,
of love, of faith, of prayer, of success,
of light, of sweetness,
of kindness, of childlike trust,
of miracles, of farming,
of diamonds, jewels,
freshness, Godliness, greatness,
power, stamina, salvation,
peace, joy, justice,
enjoyment and rebirth.

Let's sit down, don't ever frown
Just listen to your heart's crown then start over
Turn over a new page

Forget the rage . . . Let's live in peace . . .
with faith, hope and charity.

I need a lifing . . .
I need to navigate out . . .
Yes, I see a new route
Perhaps, I can run through this travail quickly . . .
Lord lift me out now

Let me sense your healing light,
for my emotions and suspicions
In the presence of the Lord is the fullness of joy,
I need a new key to my psyche

I want to scale up the charts of new endeavors
New situations,
New endowments
Therefore, I am victorious,
I am living abundantly
I am prosperous

I am whole again
Nothing shall be impossible for me
Only sweetness will drip from my lips
I can now put a lid on acrimony

I can now put a stopper on life's dross.
Because, I can look to the cross
and experience full salvation
both now and forever more
ALL things are possible if you believe

AMEN

My Grandson Troy

You stand so tall
Troy, you must get up after all
Even if you are with your friends at the mall
and never ever stall.
You must walk . . . never crawl
When you were small you cried and cried
Now you are older, you should always laugh
You're clean, sweep away your sorrows
And you have happy tomorrows
One day you will be a father
So try not to ponder or bother:
Don't be snappy
Always try to be happy.
Troy you stand so tall in my sight
Talk to me if you are ever in a plight
Try to be the greatest man you can be
Just the way God planned it for you,

Troy, my grandson . . . You are the Greatest.!!!

The Children's Song

I want to be like a flower
I want to bloom with abundance
I want to bask in the sun and dance
I want to dance as if I were in France.

I want to dance the dance of one which is not wild
I know that I am not spoiled
Just let me lift up and prance
Let me just jump up and kiss and dance

The Children's Song

We're going to first grade
We're going to first grade
Hi Ho the derrio . . . We're going to first grade

We're learning to read and write
We're learning to read and write
Hi Ho the derrio . . . We're going to first grade

We'll learn number facts
We'll learn number facts
Hi Ho the derrio . . . We're going to first grade

We'll learn science facts
We'll learn science facts
Hi Ho the derrio . . . We're going to first grade

We'll learn to get along
We'll learn to get along
Hi Ho the derrio . . . We're going to first grade.

Where Are You Going?

I'm going to the market
I'm going with my basket
I'm going to the fair
I'll see a pretty señorita there . . .
Whose name in Clair.

Jump and dance around the town
I can see the town is brightly lit
I will see if I could get a carpet
I can hear the music . . . beating up the rustic.

Look at me . . . Just look at me
I'm enjoying life and dancing in the light fantastic
I'm dancing in the light fantastic.

Everything Is Gonna Be Alright

I know that I am special
God secured the mold after he made me
There's nobody else quite like me
I believe that I have made a difference
In my family, my community, my church and my school.
I am a creator of dreams
I am a keeper of screams
I am a pleaser of teams
I like using my good judgment
I like teaching by increment
I like forgiving and being penitent
I like working for peace
I like singing with ease
I like being brave
I like being out of my cave,
because I am not a knave or a slave
I like reading a lot

I like taking notes and to jot (down strange words)
I like to give smiles
I like to walk for miles
I like different styles
My words are all in piles.
I'll never deprive anyone of hope
I'll never slide down a slippery slope
Because I'll be standing on solid ground
For I have found Jesus and Jesus has found me.
I like doing more than I have to
I like to dance and sing
I like to wear my bling
I believe I can fly, even though I don't have a wing
I like to play tunes and swing
I'd swing to the left . . . I'd swing to the right
I'd swing in the light . . . I'd swing with all my might
Knowing that everything is gonna be ALRIGHT.

Spring Is Here

Spring is here — Smell the fresh air
Let the April showers flow
So that the May flowers could grow
Spring is for everyone — fathers, mothers,
brothers and sisters.
Can you hear the music?
Dance to the beat;
Stamp your feet; spin around
Then bend down and touch the ground
Dancing is for everyone — fathers and mothers
brothers and sisters.
God is in charge
Don't worry . . . or be sorry
Just eat your roti and curry
Let your hair hang loose
Spring is for everyone — fathers and mothers
brothers and sisters — ENJOY IT.

Ms Can Can

Ms Can Can — That's what I am
I can read . . . I can write . . . I can also light up a room
I can see . . . I like to drink tea
I can walk . . . I can talk.
Oh my, the lost is quite long, because I am so strong
I can change . . . I can rearrange . . . for sure I can run the range
It's a shame, but there are so many things I can do
I do get crazy . . . But I am not hazy.
I get dizzy and sometimes frizzy
I'm always in a tizzy

Love Is All Around

Just look out — East, West, North and South
There is beauty all around
Love can be found in around
Wherever people can be found.
My heart beats with love for you
Can't you see my love is true
My tongue salivates anew
Not just when I eat the honeydew.
Love speaks and grips
Love is in all my trips
Love is growing in my garden
Love is a true kaleidoscope of cascading colors
Moving and spreading all over the world.
Love has my head in a bind
Love is just . . . It is also has principle
Love is in the framework
of all my actions.
Love motivates us to o better everyday
Love is the medicine that heals my sin-sick soul
Love is the poultice that makes me whole
Love should be everyone's goal.

Amen,

Okay

Look at me — I am Okay
Let me be — I am Okay
You must see — That I am Okay
That's It — I am certainly Okay.
We are not always the same in every wait
But I know for sure — That I am Okay
And you could be Okay
If you put your trust in God — OKAY

Please Release Me

Please release me — Let me go
Please increase me — Give me my due
Let me rise above the noise
Let me walk into my joys.
Let me run and not grow weary
Let me cruise into my inevitable destiny
Yes, let me rise up to a new standard
I know that cannot be too hard.
Read the message on the placard
Relax, let go — God is in charge
God is in control. He will save your soul
and He will also make you whole.

Happy Mother's Day

Happy Mother's Day
today is a day to reflect
on all the splendiferous
things which you have done so far.
Today is a day to reassure yourself
that you are the Queen of Hearts
It is a starry day to change your scars to stars
It is a day to relax and review the facts.
It is a day to flee from all attacks
For there can be attacks, seen and unseen
So sit back. Don't look back! You are on the right track.
You are not slack, you are not wack!
Look at all the good that's way down inside of you
Salute yourself. Get off that shelf
It's time to scale up the majestic heights of success, peace and love
Oh Yes! Love is a long beautiful ladder.
It can bubble over like a bladder
Let your fears scatter
Let the unknown chatter
Let the colorful birds flutter.
Clean up the clutter
Get out of the gutter
Because, today is your day!
Mothers, your dues have to be paid
So, stay and pray. It's an awesome day
Mother's Day.

Love

I love you
Do you love me?
I see you
Do you see me?
I can hear you
Can you hear me squeal
I can play with you
Can you play with me.
Let's be friends
Can you be my friend?
I can spin
Will you spin with me?
Let's play this game
You will never be the same

Can You Be My Friend

Be my friend
I am on the mend
Can you be my friend?
Let's go to the end and discover a new friend.
Let's skip together; let's fly off like birds of a feather
Can we play tag?
Would you get in a bag?
Walk up; don't lag.
Keep up the pact don't lag
Do you have a rag?
Or perhaps, I can use that paper bag
Always remember, you can be my friend.

Life Is About Having Hope

Life is sweet
Organize and be neat
It is better than a treat
Life is even better when we have hope.

Life can be even better when you have dreams with your hope
Life is a song and a dance
It can pull you out of a trance
Life is about skipping, dancing and prancing.

Life is filled with fantastic music
Life is filled with rustic — the funstick
These drums are exuding the same sounds
Keep Hope Alive.

Hope is special warm feeling in the heart.
It motivates you, and gives you purpose in the universe.
It makes one feel good all over.
It makes one want to jump and shout.

It puts a smile on one's face.
Hope is the potion that keeps one working,
walking, running and winning the race.
Hope is the grace we experience,
when we are in that special place.

I Am Beautiful

I am beautiful
I am awesome
I am honest
When something is true.
I say it's true.

For day has its beauty
And so does the night
A black face has beauty
And so does a white face.

I am bright and smart
And if you got it
.I'll let you know
You have to put beauty into all you do
And there is nothing wrong in enjoying it too.

I am beautiful. Yes I am
I can fly without a wing
I can sing
I can swing
I can wear my bling
I am a child of the King.

I Will Do My Best

Yes I can . . . Yes I will . . . Yes I must
Yes I promise to do my best
God will do the rest.
I promise to work and pass my test

I want to scale the height of majestic success
I want to run the race
I want favor and grace.
I want to keep my eyes on the prize

I don't like lies . . .
I know that my dream will happen
After all I am the captain
And I've been working on it everyday

I will always pray . . .
That is the way to stay.
Because I possess all these qualities I say . . .
Yes I can.

33

We Are a Team

You and me
Me and you
Talk to me
Don't balk at me.
Do you like my dress?
Can you perceive my stress?
Give me your clothes to press
Can you see the bird in its nest?
Can you help me with my test?
I seem to be at unrest
Although I am not depressed
Come on down, dance around; don't frown.
Let's walk through the town
Run around or just dance on the ground
Chase away the barking greyhound
Exercise and keep your mind sound.
Don't worry . . . Everything is gonna be alright
The Master is in charge.

My Prayer Life

Dear Lord, I need a prayer life
I'm pushing away strife
In believe3 your word
I want harmony, not the sword
I want blessings
I don't want stressing
I want fantastic dressing
I want peace and increase
Like a river
Like a fountain
Like a mountain
Like a waterfall — in my soul.

Happy New Year

Happy New Year!
Dance and lose the snare
Let loose and show that you care
This time is the best time of the year.
Kindness and goodness are in vogue
Everybody is showing love to others,
brothers are loving sisters,
mothers are loving fathers,
So, let us refuse to quit,
Let grace shine through
Let goodness and mercy marry
Let waste and poor taste disappear.
Turn over a new leaf,
Give out the sheaf,
Create a new relief
Sing a new song.
Change the crooked to the strong,

Let joy fill the world,
Let freshness pervade the atmosphere.
Let the children dance the unending foxtrot
Dance parents, dance
Lull yourself out of the trance
Reconfiigure some new constellations.
Regenerate a new thinking,
Restructure a new thinking,
Restructure a new framework for economic prowess
Success is the dress.
The testimony comes after the test
Good, better, best. Never let it rest,
Until you make your good better and your better best,
All things are possible , , , If you just believe.

35

Printed in the United States
By Bookmasters